BLAZERS

AWESOME
SPECIAL EFFECTS

EXPLOSIVE
SCENES

FIREBALLS, FURIOUS STORMS, AND MORE LIVE SPECIAL EFFECTS

BY DANIELLE S. HAMMELEF

Content Consultant:
Mira LaCous
President
Hollywood Pyrotechnics, Inc.

Reading Consultant:
Barbara J. Fox
Professor Emerita
North Carolina State University

CAPSTONE PRESS
a capstone imprint

Blazers Books are published by Capstone Press,
1710 Roe Crest Drive, North Mankato, Minnesota 56003
www.capstonepub.com

Library of Congress Cataloging-in-Publication Data
Hammelef, Danielle S.
Explosive scenes : fireballs, furious storms, and more live special effects / by
Danielle S Hammelef.)
      pages cm. — (Awesome special effects)
Summary: "Explains how physical special effects are used in movies"—Provided
by publisher.
ISBN 978-1-4914-2003-4 (library binding)
ISBN 978-1-4914-2180-2 (eBook PDF)
1. Cinematography—Special effects—Juvenile literature. I. Title.
TR858.H3523 2015
778.5'3—dc23   2014030282

Editorial Credits
Brenda Haugen, editor; Aruna Rangarajan, designer; Jo Miller, media researcher;
Tori Abraham, production specialist

Photo Credits
Alamy: AF Archive, 29, David White, 21, Jeff Morgan 07, 25, Moviestore
Collection Ltd, 17, Photos 12/Archives du 7eme Art, 15, Richard Levine, 19, Roger
Bamber, 12, YAY Media AS/Creatista, 11; Glow Images: Stocktrek Images RF, 9;
Newscom: DIMENSION FILMS/A BAND APART/BIG TALK PRODUCTIONS/
DARTMOUTH/Album, 7, Getty Images/AFP/Ali Dia, cover; The Kobal
Collection: AIP/Ridley, Laurie, 4, MGM, 23, 26

Design Elements
Shutterstock: Canicula, donatas1205, Eliks, escova, freelanceartist, ilolab, Janaka
Dharmasena, Matusciac Alexandru, NikolayPetrovich, Petr Vaclavek, Ron Dale

Printed in the United States of America in
Stevens Point, Wisconsin
092014   008479WZS15

TABLE OF CONTENTS

LET'S GET REAL!

Movie characters escape from burning skyscrapers. They run from deadly tornadoes. Explosions rock movie sets. Special effects create believable action scenes and keep actors safe.

special effect—a misleading image created for movies by using makeup, special props, camera systems, computer graphics, and other methods

LIGHTS, CAMERA—FIRE!

Special effects workers set safe and controlled fires. They use **flame bars** of different shapes and sizes. Flame bars are set around trains, buildings, and movie sets so they seem to be on fire.

Fire usually spreads up. In *Independence Day* (1996), fire spread sideways along city streets. To create this effect, a **model** of the city was made and tipped on its side.

flame bar—a metal tube filled with holes; fuel is pumped through the tube and lit to create flames

model—something that is made to look like a person, animal, or object

BEHIND THE SMOKE

How can smoke pour out of a building when there is no fire? Smoke machines are put behind the windows of buildings. The machines boil oil and release oil **vapor** into the air. The air cools the vapor and creates clouds of white smoke.

vapor—a gas made from a liquid or a solid

FACT

Bright lights behind smoke machines make it look like fires are burning.

Fire and smoke can make battle scenes more exciting. >>>

BLOWN TO BITS

Pyrotechnicians create explosions. They pack gunpowder into containers. The more gunpowder that is packed into a container, the bigger the blast. Pyrotechnicians use remote controls to set off explosions from a safe distance.

pyrotechnician—a person who is specially trained to create safe, controlled fires and explosions

remote control—a device used to make things happen from a distance

FACT

Pyrotechnicians make car explosions more exciting by loosening doors and hoods. They also remove engines and gas tanks.

Blowing real buildings into bits makes for exciting scenes. Special effects workers use models when they can't blow up real buildings. The models are filmed up close to make them seem life-sized.

WINDY WEATHER

Movie makers use fans to create windy weather. Small fans ruffle actors' hair and costumes. Larger fans make fast winds that overturn furniture. Workers throw dust or leaves into the wind to show its strength and speed.

FACT

Jet engines produced the high winds of the tornado in the 1996 movie *Twister*. Crews tossed pieces of foam into the wind to imitate trash flying in the tornado.

SPRINKLES AND STORMS

Rain can be made on movie sets. Water falls through holes in pipes above actor's heads. Workers also use rain stands, which act like big lawn sprinklers. Water goes through small holes in rain stands to make light rain. Larger holes spray bigger raindrops.

FACT

Lights and speakers plugged into a control box create lightning and thunder effects. The box triggers the lights to flash when the recorded thunder crashes.

FROM FLURRIES TO BLIZZARDS

Snow in winter scenes is made from paper, plastic, or foam. Most movies use paper snow because it lasts longer than real snow. Huge machines shred paper to give it jagged edges. Torn paper clumps together like snow.

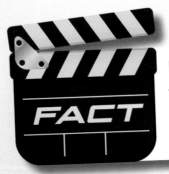

FACT Long ago workers used cornflakes to create fake snow for movies. The workers painted the cornflakes white.

19

CREEPING FOG

Movie directors sometimes use fake fog to create scary scenes. Creepy fog is made with **dry ice**. Solid dry ice turns into a gas when it warms. The gas forms a foglike cloud that hugs the ground.

dry ice—a solid form of carbon dioxide used to keep things very cold

FACT

Workers handle dry ice with gloves. People can be injured by touching dry ice because it is so cold.

MADE TO BREAK

Actors smash through doors. Tables and chairs break when heroes toss bad guys into them. These movie **props** look real, but they are built to break easily. Even sitting or leaning on these props can destroy them.

prop—an item used by an actor or performer during a show

FACT Workers also make fake glass bottles that break easily. Real glass props are used for close-ups shots when actors are drinking or eating.

CLAY IN MOTION

Artists use soft clay to make
3-D characters. Bendable metal
frames act as the clay characters'
skeletons. Clay is sometimes used
to create movie monsters.

3-D—having three dimensions:
length, width, and depth

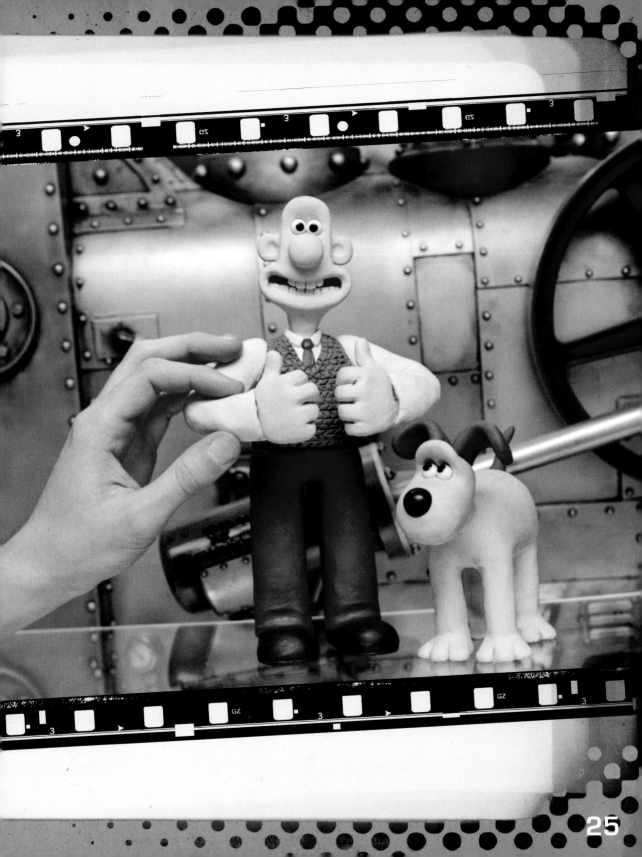

Stop-motion animation makes 3-D characters come to life. Artists make small changes to the position of a character's arms and legs. A picture is taken after each small change. When the pictures are shown together quickly, a character seems to be moving!

animation—a way of making movies by using a series of drawings or pictures and quickly presenting them, one after another, so that the characters seem to be moving

FACT

Most people can look at about 20 pictures per second and still see them as separate images. Pictures that move faster trick our eyes into seeing continuous motion.

CATCHING THE ACTION

Movie fires burn without destroying a single building. Blizzards appear on command. From exploding cars to dancing clay characters, special effects make movies fun!

A huge wave destroys a resort and more in the 2012 movie *The Impossible*. The effect was created in a giant pool with a model of the seashore and buildings.

GLOSSARY

3-D (THREE DEE)—having three dimensions: length, width, and depth

animation (a-nuh-MAY-shuhn)—a way of making movies by using a series of drawings or pictures and quickly presenting them, one after another, so that the characters seem to be moving

dry ice (DRY EYESS)—a solid form of carbon dioxide used to keep things very cold

flame bar (FLAYM BAHR)—a metal tube filled with holes; fuel is pumped through the tube and lit to create flames

model (MOD-uhl)—something that is made to look like a person, animal, or object

prop (PROP)—an item used by an actor or performer during a show

pyrotechnician (PYE-roh-tek-nih-shuhn)—a person who is specially trained to create safe, controlled fires and explosions

remote control (ri-MOHT kuhn-TROHL)—a device used to make things happen from a distance

special effect (SPESH-uhl uh-FEKT)—a misleading image created for movies by using makeup, special props, camera systems, computer graphics, and other methods

vapor (VAY-pur)—a gas made from a liquid or a solid

READ MORE

Cohn, Jessica. *Animator*. Cool Careers. Pleasantville, N.Y.: Gareth Stevens Pub., 2010.

Miles, Liz. *Movie Special Effects*. Culture in Action. Chicago: Raintree, 2010.

Mullins, Matt. *Special Effects Technician*. Cool Arts Careers. Ann Arbor, Mich.: Cherry Lake Pub., 2012.

INTERNET SITES

FactHound offers a safe, fun way to find Internet sites related to this book. All of the sites on FactHound have been researched by our staff.

Here's all you do:

Visit *www.facthound.com*

Type in this code: 9781491420034

Check out projects, games and lots more at
www.capstonekids.com

INDEX